CONTENTS

REPORTS 42

LETTERS 59

INTRODUCTION

There are now Directed Writing exercises on most examination papers. They are good tests of language ability.

'Directed Writing' is writing in which you are 'directed' by instructions which tell you how to use the information you are given. You may be asked to write a letter (formal or personal), a speech (formal or informal) or a report (sometimes called an account). You may also be asked to write a summary — either the traditional kind, where you shorten a passage, or the more modern kind, where you select only some points from the material given.

Directed Writing is also writing that is directed at a particular audience or reader, and you need to show that you can change your style and tone for that special listener or reader. 'Style' means the way you write, the kind of words and phrases you choose. The 'tone' you use for the listener or reader shows how you feel about them.

The information you are given in an exercise may include pictures, diagrams, charts or graphs as well as written material. You need to study it carefully before writing your answer as directed. You do not need to add ideas of your own to the information you are given, and in fact you may lose marks if you do so.

Over to You gives you practice in Directed Writing. There are four sections: Speeches, Summaries, Reports and Letters. In each section you will find worked answers to give you guidance, as well as other tips on how to set about particular exercises. Mark schemes are suggested to help you to assess your own work. *Over to You* gives you something to say to a particular person or persons, and will help you to say it clearly and effectively.

SPEECHES

In writing a speech, remember the following points:

- You *must* bear your audience in mind. This may be one person, a council, a committee, a school, a club or a public meeting.

- Address the audience.
  For example: 'Ladies and gentlemen, I wish to speak about ...'
  'Members of the road safety committee, I intend to draw your attention to ...'

- Begin with a simple, clear sentence announcing the subject of the speech.

- You will need to adapt the style to your audience.

- Do not just copy parts of the information given. Write it in your own words. If possible, replace words and phrases used in the text with alternatives.

- Notice carefully whether you are asked to try to persuade your audience to take a particular point of view, or just to present them with the facts.

- You will be given the information you need for the subject of the speech. Do not add your own ideas to this.

- Rearrange the facts and arguments in the order you think appropriate.

- Be strong, clear and confident in your style and presentation.

- Be careful with paragraphing. Keep one aspect of the subject to one paragraph.

- Write your final version in correctly constructed and punctuated sentences.

- Although you will be writing *as if* you are speaking, in examination answers and in the following exercises your answers are, of course, written.

1 Cowboys

Read this information and then write a speech, following the instructions you are given. The speech has been started for you, and a mark scheme has been provided, so that you may complete the exercise and see how the marks are awarded.

The cowboy of the American Wild West is a figure who has been much glamorised in films and books. But the real-life cowboy was not always the same as the legend.

Legend

Here is part of a story about a young cowboy, Jess, who has asked a ranch-owner, Joe, for a job.

Joe leaned on the corral fence and let long, silent seconds elapse while the full weight of his sinewy body settled onto his calloused elbows. His eyes narrowed to slits, just as they always did as he looked against sun and wind into the long distance of the Wyoming prairie. He had to weigh up this boy, who had ridden up and asked for a job — helping to drive two thousand of Joe's longhorn cattle from the vast plain of this mid-west state, over the Blue Ridge mountains to the cattle market to be held on the east coast in the late Fall. It was 1874, and now that the

2

cattle trade was making big money, there were any number of these youngsters about. They had bought their first horse, gun and hip holster, and were out to make a fast buck.

Joe paid his men well. Of course, most of them squandered the money on hard living before heading west again. They drank and gambled in the saloons all day and enjoyed the glamorous women who waited at the end of every trail. But Joe did not mind paying well for good men. He had worked on the trail for ten years himself, and knew how hard the job was: the hunger and thirst, the attacks by Indians, the constant fights with gun or fist. He had saved his money and built up his herd, but he was the exception. Now, he employed hard, robust men with alert minds and perfect eyesight. They had to be able to take any amount of hardship without flinching.

'Which horse would you pick from that bunch, boy?' he asked. The boy's choice would show his knowledge. Joe needed men who were natural horsemen, who could almost sleep in the saddle. Any sign of neglecting or ill-treating a horse, and he would send a man on his way. His horses were too valuable.

'I'd take the grey mare,' said Jess.

A good choice, thought Joe, but the boy could not have just what he wanted. That was not good for discipline. The boy would work under Joe's veteran foreman. Slim would teach him all he knew, but only if Jess was willing to learn, and only if he could take orders.

'Not for you, son,' said Joe. 'You'll have the black gelding in the corner over there if I decide to hire you.' After a pause, he said, 'What do you make of this?' He handed Jess a folded paper. Jess opened it. There were two dollar notes inside.

'You left these in,' Jess said. He handed them to Joe and looked straight into his eyes.

'Yeah? Thanks. What about the bill?' Those notes were the second test. It was an old trick Joe loved to play. If a man did not mention the money immediately, Joe knew he wasn't honest. All his cowboys were decent, honest men: men whom he could trust to represent him.

'It's a bill of sale for five hundred head,' said Jess. 'It's signed. It seems all right.'

'Okay,' said Joe. He needed men with their wits about them, who knew the law of cattle-trading, and the rights of both cattlemen and settlers. He needed men who wouldn't be swindled in any financial deal.

'Are you loaded?' he asked, nodding slightly towards the well-oiled revolver resting at Jess's hip. His nod was returned. Jess guessed what would happen next.

'Safety-catch off!' snapped Joe, as he tossed a bottle fifteen feet in the air. Jess showed his nerve. He didn't move for three seconds, until the bottle was at the top of its flight, the one still point in its travel. Then he drew, and shattered the bottle in one smooth movement. Joe noticed he held the gun low, close to the hip. That needed wrists and forearms as strong as iron. Joe thought this boy would get the job.

Reality

This passage is adapted from a book entitled *America: The Pioneers*.

Most cowboys were dirty, overworked and underpaid labourers who worked in terrible conditions. The climate was too hot, the land barren, and the cattle were stupid and panic-prone.

Many cowboys were Mexican, Indian or discharged Confederate soldiers. Some did break in wild horses but not many of them had their own horse. Obviously, the cowboy had to be an excellent horseman.

Cowboys were not educated. There were few schools. The cowboys would probably be able to draw and do simple arithmetic, but they were normally illiterate.

Cowboys were employed in large numbers only after the Civil War (1865 to 1885). There were about 40,000 of them in all. They drove great herds of between 500 and 2500 longhorn cattle from the great central plain to the markets in the east; at home the cattle were worth four dollars each, but at the sale, they fetched fifty dollars each. During the three or four months it took to ride about 1800 miles, the cowboy would work seven days a week for eighteen hours a day, with little food or sleep.

For the long trail the cowboy would get paid only 100 dollars — hardly enough for a new hat and boots. He certainly had the comradeship of the trail. It was a great adventure and challenge. When on the range, he lived in a bunkhouse: a wooden slum, stinking of sweat, cow manure, boots and the smoke from tallow lamps.

The average cowboy was twenty-four and he worked on average seven years before settling down on his own ranch.

Cowboys knew of the romantic associations of guns, but could not handle them and did not wear them, for they got in the way when they were riding and working. No one can shoot accurately from the hip.

There was no code of morality. Any man who survived on the great plains had to look after himself. No one else mattered. Cowboys were proud men, who did not complain, though it was a very hard life. They were caught in fires, thrown and kicked by horses, charged by cows, and many of them died of pneumonia brought on by the extremes of the weather. Each long drive was toil and trouble. Cattle drowned at river-crossings. Settlers with guns would drive the herds away from their land. The cattle never had enough water — the cowboys never had enough sleep.

The cowboy was always on the move and simply did not meet the very few girls that there were. After the long trail, when the town lights were in sight, what he longed for was not a drink or a woman — but a bath.

What you have to do

Imagine that you have been invited to speak at a Country and Western club on the topic: 'The cowboy — the legend and the reality.'

Write your speech, selecting and arranging the above material as you think appropriate. Do *not* deal with the legend first and then the reality. Compare them point by point through your speech.

✸ Worked answer

You might begin like this. (Remember to follow the guidelines given on page 1.)

Ladies and gentlemen, I have been invited by the club to compare the legend of the cowboy, as it has been glamorously portrayed to us in book and film, with the real facts of the historical cowboy as he existed in the nineteenth century on the plains of mid-west America.

Unfortunately, I must tell you that the legend is much more attractive than the reality. The traditional cowboy was a true American of the highest moral principles. In fact, most cowboys were foreigners or discharged soldiers who could find no other employment. The cowboy is usually shown handling his horse with great skill and affection, never neglecting or ill-treating it. Although cowboys had to be skilled horsemen, very few actually owned their horses. They had to do their best with the animals supplied by their employers . . .

Mark scheme

You should deal with the material by making comparisons. Give yourself 1 mark for each of the following 10 comparisons. If you have given just a list of points give half a mark for each. (The pair-comparisons make the speech more interesting and easier to follow.)

Legend	Reality
1 American	foreigner or soldier
2 affection for and skill with horses	skilled, but did not own horse
3 shrewd in matters of finance and law	illiterate, uneducated
4 raised cattle and drove them to market	there were great drives, but they were bad for cowboys
5 generous, hard-living, big spender	had comradeship of the trail, but living was squalid
6 long, healthy life of veterans and youngsters	average age 24, worked only 7 years
7 expert in drawing gun and shooting, gun a symbol of power	could not use guns, did not wear them
8 a man of honour and fair play	no honour, only self-interest and survival
9 unflinching bravery	brave and uncomplaining about the hard life
10 womaniser	no girls available, and preferred a bath

So there are 10 marks for facts if properly arranged.

Give yourself a second mark out of 10 for the style of the speech, in particular for the use of your own words, a sense of balance and contrast in the arrangement, and a sense of humour. Add these two marks for a total out of 20.

2 Petrol tanker crash

Read this information and then write a speech following the instructions on page 10.

At 2.30 p.m. on Wednesday 3 February, a petrol tanker went out of control in Windsor Road, Brinton, and, after hitting two parked cars, crossed a small front garden and partly demolished the front wall of Mr Seeley's house, No. 24, Windsor Road. The road is fairly narrow and most residents leave their cars parked in front of their houses.

Here is a plan of the area, showing the path of the petrol tanker.

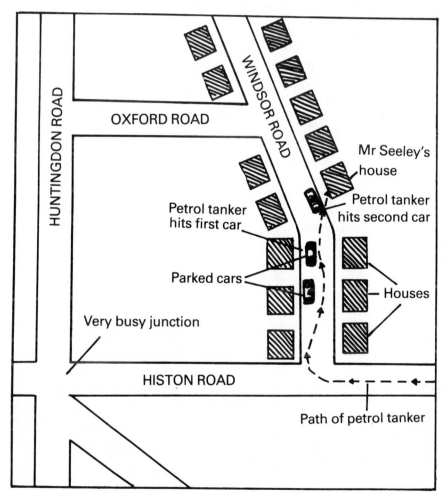

Radio Brinton covered the incident in its local news programme. Here is a transcript of on-the-spot interviews with local residents.

Interviewer Mr Seeley, what time did all this take place?

Mr Seeley It was just half-past two. I was in the back garden, when I heard this tremendous bang at the front of the house. When I went round to look, there was this petrol tanker half-way into the front room. Luckily, my wife was out. It would have killed her if she'd been in the front room.

Interviewer What will you do now?

Mr Seeley We'll have to go and stay with neighbours while the house is repaired. This has caused about three thousand pounds' worth of damage.

Interviewer Mrs Turner, you live opposite. What did you see?

Mrs Turner I heard a bang as the tanker hit our car parked outside the house. Then there was another bang, which must have been Mr Seeley's car, and then an almighty bang like an explosion. These tankers pound up and down here at all hours of the day and night. It's a miracle no one's been killed. The road isn't built to take them. It's only a residential road built to take light traffic. It's too narrow.

Interviewer What damage has been done in the past?

Mrs Turner One of the tankers demolished a telegraph pole last year, and my 'phone was put out of action.

Interviewer Have you tried to get anything done about it?

Mrs Turner Oh, yes. We've been on to the police and the council about stopping the tankers, but they won't do anything.

Interviewer Mrs Bowyer, you live nearby and have young children, I believe. What effect does all this have on them?

Mrs Bowyer None of the mothers dare let their children play out in the road. I have to keep my three-year-old boy in the house. The road isn't built for heavy lorries. It's a short-cut, of course. That's why they use it. You can feel the house shake when they go by. Cars have to be left in the road because most people don't have a drive or a garage.

Here is the article which appeared on the front page of the local evening paper.

TANKER SMASHES HOUSE

A petrol tanker went out of control in Windsor Road this afternoon and ended up in the front room of No. 24.

When questioned, a police officer said: 'The occupants of nearby houses were evacuated because of the risk of explosion, but have now returned home. The tanker has been unloaded and taken away. It is not in our power to close Windsor Road to heavy traffic. That is a matter for Brinton District Council Planning Committee.'

The driver, Mr Vic Chambers, who was detained in hospital, said that he used Windsor Road as a short-cut from Histon Road to Huntingdon Road because it cut out two junctions which had become bottlenecks. 'In my opinion,' he said, 'the western side of town should have a proper ring road, and then we wouldn't be forced to use roads like this one.'

A spokesperson for the owners of the tanker, Cleveland Oil Company, said: 'Of course there was a danger of explosion, but the fire brigade dealt with the incident. The tanker's load has been transferred to another, and the tanker in question has been taken for repair. We are glad to say that our driver will soon be discharged from hospital.

'The Company's insurers will pay for all damage to the house and we shall pay compensation to Mr and Mrs Seeley. We shall hold our own inquiry into the incident, and we apologise for any inconvenience.

'We know that our drivers travel along Windsor Road regularly. We do not dictate routes to them. If the traffic situation in Brinton was eased by the construction of a by-pass or at least a ring road, our drivers would not have to use such roads.'

What you have to do

Make a list of the main complaints of the residents of Windsor Road, and use these to write the speech a local councillor might make to the Brinton District Council Planning Committee, arguing the need for a by-pass and proposing to close Windsor Road to heavy traffic.

Mark scheme

The residents make 10 points. Check that you have covered all 10, and give yourself 1 mark for each.

Then look at the way in which you have presented the facts. Give yourself a mark out of 10 for making the link between the complaints and the need to close the road to heavy traffic, and showing that the residents, the driver, and the Cleveland Oil Company all want a by-pass.

3 A case of cruelty?

The following extract is from the court recordings of a trial in which a security firm is accused of causing guard dog puppies unnecessary suffering and cruelty. Mr Bagshaw, a member of the Dog Lovers' Association, says this in evidence:

'On the evening of Friday 10 June, I was invited by Mr Jones, a farm-worker whose isolated cottage overlooks the place concerned, to witness from his bedroom window a training session for guard dog puppies used by a security firm. He said similar training sessions took place about once a month, and what happened upset him and his family, as they considered it cruel.

The session took place in a small, deserted quarry which was enclosed by sheer rock on three sides and by a wire-netting fence, in which there was a gate, on the fourth side.

Every ten minutes an Alsatian puppy, about half-grown, was put into this compound. Then three men went into the compound, dressed in very dirty old clothes. One had a pole about four feet long with a spike on the end, and one had a short whip. These two men spent some time prodding the puppy with the spike, and darting forwards, whipping it, and then retreating. The third man, wearing heavy boots, occasionally approached the puppy and kicked it. The puppy alternately snarled at and tried to attack the men, and then ran for cover, whimpering and squealing, only to find there was none, and it then had to turn to face the advancing men again.

This happened to six puppies in turn. They tried to bite and snarl at the spike, with the result that their mouths and tongues were cut and bleeding by the end of the session. Watching through binoculars, I could detect blood on other parts of their coats by the time the ordeal was over. The men easily fended off the puppies' attacks and were deliberately brutal and merciless.

At the end, all the dogs were driven away in a large van and the men departed in cars. The puppies are destined for free-roaming guard duty wherever the firm is employed, and I can only assume that this practice is meant to make them vicious and liable to attack any intruders in their compound in the future. In my view, however, this type of training, which is not used by the armed forces, the police or reputable security firms, causes an unnecessary amount of distress, cruelty and suffering to the dogs.'

A spokesman for the firm said this in evidence:

'What Mr Bagshaw and Mr James witnessed was a standard training session for potential guard dogs.

The men wore scruffy old clothes because their arms and legs were heavily padded for protection underneath. A dog undergoes this training session only once, and it is enough to make it sufficiently fierce towards intruders. Some dogs are made too timid by it and these are discarded as being unsuitable for our purposes.

It may seem cruel to an ordinary member of the public who has not seen it before but, as I say, it happens only once to each dog, and physically the dogs quickly recover. Mentally, it equips them to do their job properly. It is no good having a guard dog which is soft or lazy and will not attack an intruder on sight. For the rest of its life, the dog will associate every intruder other than its master with this harsh treatment. A guard dog can be fed and looked after and treated kindly by only one man, its master. It always obeys its master and shows him affection. It does this for no one else, and I am afraid that is how it has got to be.

We have found this training most effective. After one ten-minute session of harsh treatment, the dog is equipped to do a lifetime's useful work in the service of the firm and the community in general.'

What you have to do

Because of its importance, the accused firm has chosen to have this case tried by a jury. Imagine that you are the judge who, having listened to the evidence, has to give a summing-up speech to the jury. Summarise the facts and the issues, and be careful to be fair to both sides.

It might be helpful to divide a page in half, and list on the left, the points made by the prosecution (Mr Bagshaw's evidence), and on the right, the points made by the accused (the firm).

Mark scheme

You should be able to find 6 points for each side. Each point carries 1 mark.

This leaves 8 marks for the judge's speech. He or she must provide the necessary factual information, balance the points and give the jury clear directions at the end.

---

4 Kidnapped

Imagine that you are a Chief Inspector in charge of the following case of kidnapping. This is the situation so far:

A twelve-year-old boy has been kidnapped from near his home. The kidnappers have telephoned his father, a wealthy banker, at home, to say that they want £200,000 in used bank notes, or he will not see his son again. They have sent proof that they have his son.

He has been instructed to go to several public telephone boxes, which he has done, getting fresh instructions in each. He now has a brown-paper parcel containing the money, and has been ordered to leave it in the litter bin in the corner of the car park, shown in the plan, at 7 p.m. on Tuesday. He has kept the police informed at each step, though he was warned by the kidnappers not to tell them.

The need to keep out of sight is obvious. You can have as many officers to help as you wish. As the father has not been ordered to go to another telephone box, you are sure that this time the kidnappers are going to collect the money. If the kidnappers have the boy with them and release him as soon as they have the money, you can, of course, close in and arrest them. But they will probably take the money and, if satisfied, release the boy later. All you can do at the car park is to hide, watch and try to identify the collectors of the money and any car they may use.

You have assembled your officers and you have to give them instructions. You will need to make use of all cover such as cars, trees, fences, and so on. You also decide to make use of disguise and impersonation.

What you have to do

Referring to the plan, tell the officers clearly what the situation is, where you want them to hide, wait and watch, and what other action to take if possible.

Do not add ideas that cannot be deduced from the information.

Do not make the instructions too long.

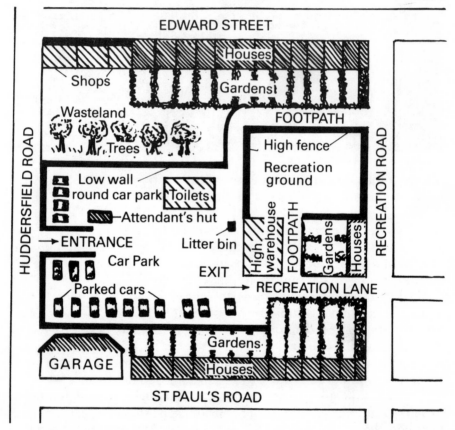

Mark scheme

To judge how good your answer is, work out a scheme based on the balance of marks that has been suggested for the first three exercises.

5 Tricars

The notes that follow have been made by a Member of Parliament who intends to make a speech in Parliament about changes in government policy concerning 'tricars', which are three-wheeled cars supplied to disabled drivers.

DHSS (Department of Health and Social Security)

- Has supplied and maintained tricars for 21,000 disabled people
- Will not now do this
- Instead grants 'mobility allowance' of £5 per week

Jill Eyre (tricar driver and Secretary of National Association of Disabled Drivers) says:

- £5 per week isn't enough
- You can't buy, tax and insure a car for £5 per week
- It will cost government £260 a year for each disabled driver's tricar
- But if they don't have tricars they can't get to work
- Government will lose about £1000 per year in income tax and national insurance contributions from each working driver
- Government will have to pay disabled drivers unemployment pay - £750 p.a. each
- Scheme will cost government over £2000 for each disabled driver who can't now work
- If they all worked, government would save £42 million per year

Ron James (a famous rally driver) tested tricar and says:

- Turning-circle is too small to be safe
- It's easy to turn car over
- Car is unstable and dangerous
- Car could easily catch fire

Eric Ward (tricar driver) says he couldn't cope without tricar:

- Needs it to get to work
- Couldn't go shopping, to football matches or anywhere without it
- Thinks the government wants to forget disabled drivers
- Has found tricar very reliable - it's never let him down
- Tricar got him about when other cars were stuck in ice and snow
- Allowance of £5 per week is a sick joke

What you have to do

Write the MP's speech in clear, correct sentences, arranging the above material in whatever way you think appropriate. Argue for keeping tricars for disabled drivers, and attack the government's policy of replacing them with a £5 a week allowance. Be very careful not to introduce any of your own ideas.

6 Dog licences

Your local radio station has arranged a discussion about the proposal to increase the cost of a dog licence to £10 a year.

One speaker, Mr Johnson, has made the following points in favour of increasing the cost:

- Too many dogs are allowed to roam the streets out of control — the new fee would reduce their number
- They cause many road accidents
- They cause inconvenience and a hazard to health by soiling pavements, parks and other public places
- They cause financial loss to many farmers by worrying and killing sheep

You are invited to reply to Mr Johnson. You have with you a leaflet published by the Dog Defence League which makes the following points:

- Of the hundreds of thousands of dogs kept as pets, 50% are owned by children under 16, and 25% by elderly people
- Dogs give a feeling of security to elderly people and men and women living alone
- Hundreds of dogs earn their living by working for the police, the armed forces, shepherds, farmers, security firms and blind people
- Dogs are an important source of sporting pleasure
- The dog-breeding industry earns valuable foreign currency with its many exports
- The dog food industry employs thousands of people

What you have to do

Make a speech urging that dog licence costs remain the same. Use the information from the leaflet as you think appropriate and answer Mr Johnson's points.

7 Land development

As the father or mother of two small boys, you are going to attend a public meeting, arranged by the local council, to hear people's views about the use of a piece of derelict land near where you live. The land is owned by the council. It has not yet been decided whether it should be sold to a local builder, Barnett & Sons Ltd, who would build houses on it, or turned into a children's play area.

Below is a list of points you have made in preparation for making a speech at this meeting, in favour of a play area:

- A play area would benefit the whole community, in which there are many children
- Many children already play on the land in its derelict state and would have nowhere else to play if it was built on
- Without a play area, there could be more vandalism of bus shelters, telephone boxes, parks etc.
- A set of goalposts and a grass area would be more useful than flower beds and lawns
- A slide, swings, paddling pool and climbing bars would attract younger children
- An adventure playground would need a higher climbing structure, ropes, large tyres etc.
- To make it a properly finished job, carefully positioned logs and landscaped hillocks and ravines would be needed

What you have to do

Write the speech you intend to make at the public meeting, using the above information as you think appropriate.

Begin: 'Chairperson, ladies and gentlemen ...'

SUMMARIES

A summary is a short report. In all jobs where reports have to be written, information has to be summarised. People studying for examinations take notes, and in this way summarise talks, lectures, demonstrations, experiments, articles, essays or books. A newspaper is a summary of the day's news. We all summarise in everyday conversation. If we describe something to a friend — a football match, a film, a book, a television programme — we summarise the main points.

To prepare a summary, you must take in the main ideas or facts of a piece, and then rewrite them briefly in your own words. This tests your ability to distinguish what is important from what is not important.

You will be told how long your summary should be. There are three main stages:

1 Understanding what is read.
2 Selecting what is important.
3 Rewriting the important ideas in your own words.

This is what you do:

1 Read the original passage 3 or 4 times to absorb it thoroughly.
2 Make notes. There are two reasons for doing this:
   (a) If you think the final version may be too long, you can decide which ideas are less important, and cut out some of them.
   (b) You are more likely to use your own words if you are writing up notes than if you are working directly from the passage.
3 Write a draft in complete sentences from the notes.
4 If the draft is too long, cross out words and phrases until it is short enough. You may even have to start again.
5 If the draft is too short, check to see if you have missed any important ideas.

6 When the length of the draft is about right, write the final form of the summary in complete sentences, as fluently as possible.

7 Make sure your final version is one *coherent* passage.

Remember:

- Any direct speech in the original must be put into reported form.
- Marks will be lost if the summary is too long.
- Marks may be lost for copying phrases from the original; use your own words, replacing words and phrases from the original with alternatives.
- Sometimes your final summary will have the ideas in the same order as the original, but at other times you may have to rearrange points.
- Use only the material given. Do not add your own ideas or opinions.

The first summary has been done for you, and a mark scheme provided. This shows you how to *shorten* a passage by expressing the essential points.

The third summary, a *selective* one, has been started for you and a mark scheme provided.

8 Crash landing

Read the following passage and then summarise it in not more than 115 words.

Night had fallen as we crossed the mountains and before long, far away below us, we saw the River Chindwin, and knew that we were over Japanese-occupied territory. We had been airborne for an hour and a half when the glider was shaken by a violent gust of wind. All the loose stores and equipment went clattering across the floor, and the whole structure shuddered so fiercely that it seemed the glider would fall to pieces in mid-air. There was only one course open to the pilot. He cut. That is to say, he put up his right hand and punched a knob in the roof over his head, and we parted company with the plane that was towing us.

The first thing we noticed was the silence. It was so peaceful. We heard only a gentle swishing sound as we floated through the darkness. Below us in the moonlight lay a solid black carpet of jungle, towards which we were slowly and rather unsteadily descending in wide circles. At this point it looked very much as if we were doomed. There was only one small break in the black canopy of treetops — a tiny little speck of white. We made for it, swinging nearer and nearer to the earth until suddenly treetops were flicking past my window; we were through them; we were coming into a strip of sand dotted with boulders and — crash — we had landed. We had landed in the bed of a stream where it splayed out in the bottom of a gully. The nose of the glider was smashed and the pilot and I were now buried under a blasphemous mass of soldiery. Fortunately, no one was hurt.

✳ Worked answer

Your notes might look like this:

Night – mountains and River Chindwin below – over Japanese territory – $1\frac{1}{2}$ hours – glider shaken by wind – inside contents thrown around – glider might disintegrate – cut connection from towing plane – silence, peace – jungle underneath – circling down – one break – through treetops – landed in a stream – no one hurt.

Generally speaking, summaries are about one-third of the length of the original passage. In this example there are 44 words in the notes. This is about right: when expanded into full sentences they will be near the limit of 115 words. Always check back at this stage to see if you have left out any important ideas. Then you write up:

It was night. Our glider flew over mountains and the River Chindwin: this was Japanese-occupied territory. After one and a half hours' travel, the glider was shaken badly by a gust of wind. Our stores and equipment were scattered — the glider shuddered and we feared it would disintegrate. The pilot was forced to disconnect our towing glider by punching a knob in the roof overhead. We flew on in peaceful silence. However, we were circling slowly downwards, and below, there was only one small, white break in the jungle. We aimed for this, and brushing through treetops, we landed in the bed of a stream. Though there was much confusion, no one was hurt.

Mark scheme

Show marks for content by ticks in the summary:

night; crossing mountains; River Chindwin; Japanese-occupied territory; airborne for $1\frac{1}{2}$ hours; gust of wind; glider shaken; equipment scattered; structure shuddered; break-up imminent; cut from plane; silence; peace; jungle below; descending; speck of white; brushed treetops; landed in stream; chaos; no one hurt.

Give these ticks half a mark each to give a content mark out of 10. Award a mark out of 10 for the use of your own words and for the quality of your style in general, to make a total out of 20.

Then subtract 1 mark for each line of average-size writing over 115 words.

9 Camping and caravanning

Read the following passage and then summarise it in no more than 200 words.

Combine freedom, inexpensiveness and life in the countryside, and you have all the ingredients of a marvellous holiday. The way to enjoy such a holiday is by camping or caravanning.

Whether you take a van or tent to the Continent, or elect to stay in Britain, you can have a lot of fun getting close to Nature. The prime attraction is freedom of movement, although caravanners are, to a certain extent, limited in their movements around the country, by the availability of sites.

Camping in its purest form is not recommended for the casual type. You must be prepared for cramped living quarters and weather of all descriptions. You must be strong enough to carry your home, cooking utensils, sleeping equipment and goodness knows what else on your back. But once this proves acceptable, there is — as camping enthusiasts will tell you — nothing quite like it.

A step up from the mere tent is the tent-trailer or trailer-tent. This is a trailer which can be opened out into a full-sized, rigid-sided tent, with a solid base and sides.

Most people have some idea of the kind of caravan they would like to own, and modern ones with their double glazing, insulated linings, showers, loos, central heating and what-have-you make holiday-making quite a home-from-home affair. But when it comes to buying a caravan, there are a few things which should guide your choice, other than the cost. Nearly all car manufacturers state a maximum trailer weight that should be towed by their vehicles. This depends on engine power, braking power, suspension and transmission.

A caravan can be extended by using an awning. These are like large tents which fit onto the sides of the van, and provide semi-outdoor accommodation. They can be zipped up at night if you want to use them for extra sleeping room, or opened completely on one side for meals.

Of course, the cost of shipping a caravan to the Continent can be high, but averaged out between members of, say, a family of four, this can still prove a cheap holiday.

Motor caravanning can be a little deceptive compared to trailering, for the average motor caravan offers relatively cramped accommodation for not more than two adults. Only the large American-type vans, or the long-wheelbase custom vans made in this country, are really comfortable for the average family. Nevertheless, they are fun — and the most mobile camping and caravan holidays of all are to be had with them. They are perhaps best for a couple with young children, and their ample window space offers youngsters a maximum view of the countryside as they travel along. You can even see them playing games or eating snacks while Mum or Dad is driving. Motor caravans, too, can be fitted with awnings to extend living accommodation while on site, and these awnings can be left in place, zipped up, while the van is used for day tripping.

For all forms of camping and caravanning there are organisations ready to assist you with problems concerning overseas holidays, insurance, sites in Britain, regulations and so on. For campers the Camping Club of Great Britain and Ireland at 11 Grosvenor Place, London SW1. is most helpful, while caravanners can contact the Caravan Club at East Grinstead, West Sussex.

By the way, if you are wondering what any of these types of holiday are like, and don't want to lay out a lot of money buying the equipment, try hiring it for a trial period. It is possible to hire tents, sleeping equipment, cooking and dining furniture, vans and motor caravans, and just about anything that goes with them. Some firms will also sell off hired goods at the end of a season at considerable reductions.

10 Happiness

The following statements were taken from essays written by fifth-year students who were giving their opinions on what they thought they needed to be happy in life. You will find that the same ideas are repeated in several of the essays, but you need only mention them once in your summary.

1 'I want to get a job that I will enjoy doing. People spend so much of their lives working that I think it is important to enjoy what you are doing. A lot of the most unhappy people I know are people who do not like their jobs. I hope mine will be well paid, but that is not the most important thing.'

2 'I want to be successful. I want to achieve something. This is the most important thing, to feel you are doing something worthwhile. I hope I can achieve this in my job, but it might be through one of my hobbies or interests.'

3 'Good health is most important if you want to be happy. It is far more important than having a lot of money. You need enough money to get what you want, of course, but it is not the most important thing. I find it hard to imagine what it must be like to live a life of pain, or to have to take pain-killing drugs every day.'

4 'My idea of happiness is to be able to do the things that interest me. I like all kinds of sport, and especially swimming. So I will need to enjoy good health, though my sports are not very expensive.'

5 'People are most important to me. Without people around you life is not worth living. I hate being on my own. It is most important to relate to people and be kind so that they are good to you in return. And the most important relationship, of course, is with the person you marry.'

6 'A good job, a good marriage, and enough money for what you want — what more could anyone want?'

7 'I love travelling and seeing new places, so this is the great thing for me. To travel a lot, you need plenty of money, of course. Staying and living in the same town all my life is not for me — and I do not want to get tied down with family responsibilities.'

8 'In these days of high unemployment among young people, to get a job is the most important thing. It is best to get a job that you enjoy, but any job would do for me. Then you can be happy in other things.'

9 'A good marriage and plenty of sport — that will keep me happy.'

10 'A good job and the spare time to do all the things I love doing — tennis, swimming, hiking. Good health is important too, of course.'

11 'Life has been good to me so far. I have health, strength, friends, and enough money for what I want. I want to devote my life to the service of God. That would bring me true happiness and fulfilment.'

12 'I want to be successful, to succeed in my job and to feel that I am doing something worthwhile, helping people, making the world a better place. This may sound pious, but it is true. I hope to be a nurse, so I may be able to travel abroad, too.'

13 'I like family life and plenty of friends in general. What is life without friends? I would like to travel abroad, too.'

14 'To be happy, I must be a winner. I am not interested unless I win. I am an athlete, and to me, coming second is coming nowhere. I must win. I must be top of the heap. It gives me a feeling of pride and satisfaction.'

15 'Happiness to me is success in my job. I don't want just any job. I am going to be a doctor. This, for me, is a vocation. It will not be a living but a way of life. I will be dedicated to it twenty-four hours a day. The money doesn't matter. I may go to the Third World and heal the sick of poor countries. All I want to do is practise medicine and relieve suffering. I will be totally dedicated.'

What you have to do

Summarise in continuous writing the ideas that are given in these extracts. Rearrange the material in whatever way you think suitable. Write your summary in no more than 200 words.

✳ Worked answer

(This is a *selective* summary, involving more than just shortening the passage.)

Your summary could begin like this:

Many fifth-year students say that in order to be happy, they must first get a job. This is a time of high unemployment and to get any job is a first priority, with enjoyment of it, security and good pay being desirable in that order. The highest priority for others is good health, for what good would money be in a life of pain and illness? For others, the idea of success or achievement, whether in their job or through hobbies or interests, is the thing from which all others will flow ...

Mark scheme

There are 20 main factual points:

- any job
- secure job
- good health
- plenty of, or enough, money
- sense of adventure
- importance of hobbies, interests
- importance of sport
- popularity and sociability
- family life
- importance of spare time
- God and/or Church
- winning

- enjoy job
- well-paid job
- absence of pain and/or illness
- travelling
- success and achievement — through job or interests
- friends or interest in people
- good marriage
- doing something worth-while, helping people etc.

You earn half a mark for each of these factual points. Show this by ticks in the summary (i.e. mark out of 10).

Award yourself a mark out of 10 for the use of your own words and for the quality of your style in general, to make a total of 20.

Then subtract 1 mark for each line of average-size writing over 200 words.

11 Bus strike

Read the following information and then write a summary following the instructions on page 30.

Imagine that in your area the bus conductors have decided to stop work each evening at 10 p.m. because of attacks upon them after that time. Some local opinion is sympathetic to them, but other people say they are being awkward, causing unnecessary inconvenience and not doing their job properly. Suppose that you are a journalist whose job it is to write an account of local feeling on the issue. You have gone into the streets to interview people and you have collected these comments on your tape recorder:

1   'I don't blame the conductors at all. Other people can do their jobs in peace without risk of physical assault. Why shouldn't they?'

2   'Why don't they call the police and let them deal with it?'

3   'They don't get paid for taking that risk, you know. If you are a soldier or a policeman, you expect to be paid to be endangered, but not if you work on the buses.'

4   'It's just an excuse to be awkward. These unions are causing trouble again.'

5   'I live in the country. How can I have an evening in town and be back home by ten? Impossible. It means no social life for me.'

6   'I couldn't care less. I think everybody ought to be home by ten. It's only drunkards and layabouts who aren't.'

7   'I'm only fifteen and my parents tell me to be in by ten anyway.'

8   'It's disgusting. It's all right for these people with cars. How would they like to have to walk everywhere after ten o'clock?'

9   'A good thing. These bus conductors have a hard life. Shift work. Early mornings. Late nights. Up and down stairs all day. Rude passengers. They can do without being beaten up as well.'

10 'Yes. The other passengers just sit there and leave it to the conductor to deal with, don't they? Why don't they get up and help him and do something about it?'

11 'People don't deserve to have late buses if they don't support the conductor.'

12 'Drunken hooligans. There's too much of that these days. Why should they run late buses for them?'

13 'Good thing. Make them walk. Do them good.'

14 'Rubbish! It's the unions again. Too big for their boots. Stick 'em all in the army.'

15 'Don't care. I've got my motorbike.'

16 'It's the modern world, isn't it? Everything's closing down. Things just aren't the same any more.'

17 'Well, there aren't any cinemas any more, so these louts who do the assaulting must have come out of the pubs, mustn't they? Stop the buses, I say. Serve them right.'

What you have to do

This is another *selective* summary.

As a journalist, write an account of these opinions, trying to be impartial and to do justice to both sides of the argument. Do not add your own opinions and do not write in dialogue (speech) form.

Write the summary in not more than 200 words.

12 Got any cigarettes?

Here is a play script about teenage smoking.

(*A group of fourth-year pupils is standing about behind the bicycle shed at morning break.*)

Anne   Got any cigarettes? I've finished mine and I'm dying for a fag.

Cathy   The duty teacher will be round in a minute. I don't want to get caught again or I'll be in real trouble this time.
(*Chorus of jeers*)

Anne   Who cares? The teachers tell you not to smoke, but most of them do in the staffroom. I'm going to keep on smoking whatever they try to do or say to me. Some of the others have stopped though. I'll bet at the beginning of the year there would've been about a couple of dozen of us round here every morning break and afternoon break. Two terms later, and we're down to about eight or nine. That's not many out of a fourth year of about two hundred, is it?

Cathy	Well, a lot of people keep on at you these days to give up, saying it's bad for you and all that. But I don't care, because my mum says I can smoke and she gives me most of mine.
Anne	Yes, so does my mum, but most parents don't. Does anyone else get given fags by mums and dads? (*Groans of disbelief*)
Wendy	I wish I did. It's so expensive. It takes all my paper round money, and a lot more besides.
Alan	I think I'm going to give up and save up to buy a bike.
Wendy	(*laughing*) That shouldn't take long, the amount of money you send up in smoke!
Graham	I think I'll soon have to get in training for the mile on sports day. That means no smoking for the summer.
Anne	Oh, go on. What difference is a few puffs going to make? Everyone knows you'll win, anyway.
Graham	Yes, but I'm going down to the athletics club again this season and they told me last year that none of them smoke. It's not just the risk of lung cancer, they said. Smoking affects everything — the condition of your heart and circulation, your general reflexes and the amount of air your lungs can take in.
Wendy	(*sneering*) Well, that's all right for a superstar like you, but I'm hooked. It's a habit I can't get rid of. My nerves need it. How am I going to handle all that shouting and nagging I get at home, not to mention the teachers always after me, if I can't calm down with a quick fag every now and again?
Alan	You sound like my mum. She says that's why she can't give up. 'Don't think smoking will make you seem big or clever,' she says to me. 'When you get to my age and your nerves are shattered and your money runs away like water, you'll wish you'd never started.' So I think I need that bike more than poverty and a lifetime's cough. I'm off. Cheerio.
Anne	Another good man gone.

What you have to do

This play was shown on television to lead into a discussion on 'Teenagers' attitudes to smoking'. Write a summary of the ideas it contains. Do not use more than 200 words.

13 Sundays

Imagine that you are a historian and you have found a collection of diaries, some (Section A) kept by modern teenagers, all aged fifteen or sixteen, and others (Section B) by teenagers of fifty years ago. You study the diary entries for Sundays and this mixture of facts and feelings is what you find.

Section A

Julie

Sunday again. Lovely. I do absolutely nothing on Sunday and I love it. I got worn out at the shop yesterday, and didn't get home till three after the disco. So as usual I stayed in bed until lunchtime.

I woke up at ten and turned on the radio — very low so Mum wouldn't complain. I just lay there and dreamt about the disco, and about Peter. Then I smelt the lunch cooking — good old Mum. Mum doesn't mind me staying in bed. She says it keeps me out of her way and my Dad just reads the papers and drinks coffee all morning. In the afternoon, I went round to Peter's and helped him get his bike ready for next week's race. In the evening I watched television and had a bath.

Mike

My hobby is motocross and although I am not old enough to ride motorbikes on public roads yet, I have been riding for three years now and I know all about bikes and building and repairing them. I go around with Dave to motocross meetings every Sunday. It's fantastic, the best day of the week. I want to be a professional when I leave school.

Steve

I played football as usual this morning. We won. We always play on a Sunday because we watch a League match on Saturday. They can play League matches on Sunday now if they want to, but they never do round here. I felt tired in the afternoon, so I had a soak in the bath and, later on, I went round to see one of my mates.

Mandy

I was down at the pool training by 6.30. They don't open the pool to the public until ten on Sundays, so that gives us a good three hours with only us and the coach. I'm in the county team this year, and if I want to do well in the nationals, training is the only way. The rest of the day I sat around the house and played records and caught up on the homework I hadn't done in the week and watched television.

Daniel

Sunday again. It's boring. There's never anything to do round here. The place is dead. No cinemas, no discos. Mum and Dad go to church, but I don't go any more. I'm not sure if I believe in religion any more. I slept late, and then sat around reading magazines and the Sunday papers. In the afternoon I worked on the hi-fi amplifier I'm building.

Sue

I went to church as usual this morning. I can't understand people who stay in bed on a Sunday. A lot of my friends do. I say they are sleeping their lives away. They miss so much. I love to go to church and have that feeling of peace and happiness. Then I read and did some studying in the afternoon.

Lloyd

I helped Dad all day. He has so much building work on at the moment that he works seven days a week. I love helping him. I like anything practical, and I can't wait to leave school and work with him all the time. School work is so boring. I make a lot of money on a Sunday.

Section B

Mary

I went to church very early in the morning and then spent all the rest of the day riding at Molly's Dad's farm. There's nothing I love more than being with horses all the time and that's why I love Sunday.

John

Sunday again. It's the worst day of the week. I had to go to church twice. I hate going, getting all dressed up and singing boring hymns. I don't believe in God any more but I'm forced to go. I hate it. But there's nothing else to do, and you just have to sit around listening to the wireless when you're not at church.

Marion

It was a lovely Sunday today, so quiet and peaceful, and the weather was glorious. It's often a lazy day, but I read a lot today. I didn't go to church. I go sometimes, but Dad never makes me because he spends nearly all day gardening!

Edward

I stayed in bed until late and then read one of my Edgar Wallace murder stories. Mum doesn't like me reading that sort of thing on a Sunday, but I don't care. I'm too busy to read them during the rest of the week. We had visitors for tea and I had to be all dressed up and polite and on my best behaviour. I hate Sundays. It always seems to be such a stiff and starchy day. You can't play football or go to the pictures or do anything much at all.

Jean

It's been one of those special Sundays. I went walking on the moors with Dorothy and her parents. We had a picnic and didn't get back until nearly dark. They do that most Sundays and quite often ask me to go with them. I love all the fresh air and countryside and peace, but Mum and Dad don't let me go out when we have visitors.

What you have to do

Write a section of a local history magazine entitled 'Sunday today and yesterday'. Make it a summary of these diary entries. You will have to rearrange much of the material. There is no need to mention the diarists' names. Make your summary as factual as possible with only a little reference to the feelings expressed. Use the facts in Section A to make a comparison between how people used to spend Sunday fifty years ago and how they spend Sunday today.

> ## Mark scheme
>
> It might be useful in this exercise to construct your own mark scheme, based on a selection of the facts that need to be included.

one nuclear warhead
has more explosive
power than all the
bombs dropped in
World War II . . .

These four speeches were part of a school debate. The issue was 'Nuclear weapons should be abolished'. Joanne and Gary spoke in support of this statement, and Michael and Sonia spoke against it.

Joanne

The human mind cannot imagine the destructive power of a nuclear bomb. A few thousand tonnes of T.N.T. What does that mean? One warhead having more explosive power than all the bombs dropped in the Second World War. How can you imagine that? And hundreds of missiles with multiple warheads. It is beyond our understanding. This power is so enormous it cannot be controlled by people. People are weak and irrational. One mistake with this power, and the world blows up. We must banish nuclear weapons before it is too late. Do we want to destroy our civilisation?

Apart from what we destroy by the explosion, nuclear weapons contaminate the atmosphere. Radioactivity destroys all life slowly and painfully.

37

What a price we pay for these risks! Billions of pounds every year are consumed by these murderous weapons. If they were abolished, just think what uses the money could be put to — the number of hospitals that could be built, the extra care for the sick, the handicapped, the old. This is the true price we pay for nuclear weapons.

Michael

Joanne's passionate plea to save the world from destruction sounds very fine and very noble. But the trouble with Joanne and people like her is that they are dreamers. They seem blissfully unaware of the facts of life — the way people really behave.

Human beings are aggressive by nature. Other animals do not kill their own kind. Human history is the story of wars, of one war after another. History also shows that pacifism does not work. If you give way to the bully it only makes him worse. If you try to make peace with aggressive nations, they always take advantage. The Second World War would not have happened if we had stood up to Hitler earlier. We must stay strong, have all weapons at our disposal, and say we will use them in retaliation only.

The beauty of this is that no one actually will use them. No one dares actually destroy or contaminate the world. Therefore the balance of power works. Russia and America threatened each other over the Cuban Missile Crisis in 1962, and they both found a way of not firing their weapons. The Third World War was over and done with in 1962. America successfully defended the western hemisphere without a shot being fired. This is why we have had over forty years with no major wars. A nuclear bomb shortened the Second World War and saved thousands of lives in the Far East, and has prevented any major war since then.

You could say the same about germ and gas warfare. The weapons are there but no one will use them. Wars now have to be small-scale and waged with conventional weapons.

Gary

Michael's position is not logical. The fact that there has not been a war does not mean that there will not be one. And the risk is too great to run. We are making decisions not only for now, but for future generations. Must people live under the shadow of the bomb for ever?

What makes the risk greater is the possibility of nuclear weapons spreading. Probably only five countries have them now, but what if ten or twenty countries had them? We have seen madmen in power in small countries before. What if one of them had a finger on the button?

What this country needs is the moral courage to be the first to disarm. It costs nothing. If just one country showed good faith and abandoned the weapons it had, who knows who might follow? We wouldn't be attacked the next day. What have we got to lose? We could gain the salvation of the world. Why not us?

Sonia

The moral argument used by Gary applies to all weapons and not just nuclear ones. It does not work. People are aggressive. We must keep peace through strength.

Another thing to remember is that research on nuclear energy leads to all sorts of other peaceful uses of this amazing power, such as the production of electricity.

Joanne mentioned the expense. How simple can you be? The money not spent on weapons for war, if that happened, would not be spent on hospitals. There would be more useless jobs created at public expense, or taxes would be lowered and people would keep their money — money to spend on luxury electrical goods to make them lazy, or on bigger cars, or on cosmetics to satisfy their vanity. I'd rather have strong defence forces than a colour television, and I offer the same choice to you.

What you have to do

Write a summary of the ideas contained in these speeches on whether to keep or abolish nuclear weapons. Give the arguments for and against. There is no need to keep to the order in which the ideas are given in the speeches, and there is no need to refer to the speakers or to give their names.

Write the summary in not more than 200 words, and give it the title 'The problem of nuclear weapons'.

15 Working on a farm

In the part of a play which follows, Brian, a fifteen-year-old boy who works on Mr Bourne's farm on Saturdays, discusses with Jim, a farm-worker for twenty years, the prospect of working for Mr Bourne permanently.

Brian What do you think of working full-time for Mr Bourne, Jim?
Jim Well, is it what you want to do, Brian?
Brian It's all right. Can't say I'm mad about it, but at least it's a job, and you have to take what you can get these days. Those who have got jobs of any kind are lucky.
Jim There's job security all right, and Mr Bourne's a good boss.
Brian How does he pay, though? Farming doesn't pay very much, does it?

Jim	No, that's true. No one ever made a fortune from working on a farm, but it doesn't compare too badly with factory wages nowadays. Another thing is that you can get in a lot of over-time at certain times of the year, with harvesting late at night, and early morning starts.
Brian	Doesn't all that get a bit much sometimes?
Jim	It does if you don't like hard work. You usually have to do some weekends and even Bank Holidays at Easter, Christmas and New Year. It's no good taking it on if you don't like this life, being in the open air all the time.
Brian	Oh, I'd like that. I couldn't stand being shut up in a factory or an office. Farming must be much healthier.
Jim	It is. You are always in touch with Nature and you can see the changes of the seasons. That can be very satisfying. If you like practical work and work with animals, it's the right job for you.
Brian	Do you always have to live in a farm cottage?
Jim	Sometimes you do, and the trouble is that then you have to leave the house if you leave the job. The Union will get you some safeguards against being thrown out, though. Some people live in their own houses.
Brian	I bet they have to travel a long way to work, don't they?
Jim	Yes, and there's not much public transport in country areas. I think one of the best things about it is that usually you work on your own, or with just a couple of others, so there isn't always a boss or foreman harassing you.
Brian	I'd like that, too. I reckon it's the job for me.

What you have to do

Summarise the ideas in favour of and against the job of a farm-worker as described in this conversation. Rearrange the material in whatever way you think suitable. There is no need to refer to Jim or Brian.

Try to write the summary in not more than 200 words.

REPORTS

A report is a combination of narrative (a recital of events or facts) and explanation. People in many kinds of job need to write reports — engineers, journalists, police officers, social workers, secretaries, lawyers, scientists, doctors and so on. Teachers often have to write special reports — for parents, for the students' employers, for other schools and colleges, for magazines and newspapers and even for probation officers and law courts. Reports are needed for so many different uses that it is not possible to say exactly how they should be put together, but you should always bear in mind the following points:

1 Read the information you are given very carefully so that you understand it thoroughly.

2 Supply a title, even if the question does not ask for it.

3 Address the report to the person who wants it, whether this is an employer, a local government officer, a firm's customer etc.

4 Begin with a clear, simple sentence, announcing the subject of the report.

5 A report may be written in the past or present tense, but once you have chosen which you are going to use, be consistent and stick to it.

6 You do not have to keep to the original order of the ideas. Rearrange them to suit your report.

7 If you have to report any conversation, avoid using direct speech.

8 Make the report clear and accurate. Marks may be lost for wasting words. You must choose only the facts necessary for the report's purpose. Read the information provided several times. Cross out the points which have nothing to do with the purpose of the report. List the main points — these are the facts you must use clearly in your report.

9 Plan the report in paragraphs, keeping one aspect of the subject for each paragraph.

10 If the instructions ask you to give facts and to draw conclusions, separate the facts and their interpretation clearly. Be strong and confident about your conclusions.

11 You *must* write in your own words. Do not copy whole sentences from the original information, though you will not be able to avoid using some of the original words. If you can, replace words and phrases used in the passage with alternatives.

12 Write your final report in complete, properly constructed and punctuated sentences.

13 Though the number of words is not prescribed, as with summaries, it is best not to make reports too long.

14 The first report, 'Yellow peril', has been started for you, to give you an idea of the style required. A mark scheme is provided so that you may complete the exercise and see how the marks are awarded.

16 Yellow peril

Read the following four items of information and then answer the question at the end.

1 Here is a word-by-word account of how Mr Ackroyd, MP for Wilthorpe, questioned Mr Reg Thomas, the Minister for the Environment, about a matter of some concern to his constituents living near Pearson's factory in Wilthorpe.

Mr A. Is the Minister aware of the unpleasantness and danger to the health of the citizens of Wilthorpe caused by Pearson's factory, which is situated in the north of the town?

Mr T. The proximity of the factory to a residential area is unfortunate. It was built before the present planning regulations came into force.

Mr A. I know that, but I'm asking what can be done to make things more pleasant and more healthy for the residents.

Mr T. It has been reported to me that the factory does emit a moderate quantity of smoke and unpleasant fumes.

Mr A. Moderate quantity? It's billowing out all day long and every day. 'Pearson's poison' my constituents call it.

Mr T. The management is, I understand, well aware of the situation and does what it can to cut down the amount of smoke and fumes emitted, but it is partly unavoidable because of the industrial process used.

Mr A. Is Wilthorpe by law a smokeless zone?

Mr T. That applies only to domestic fires and chimneys.

Mr A. But Pearson's can poison people for their own profit?

Mr T. That is an exaggeration and a distortion. You can't close down all the factories in this country because they are smoky. The inhabitants of Wilthorpe should be thankful to firms like Pearson's for the employment and prosperity they bring to the town.

2 This is what a woman living near the factory had to say:

'Pearson's poison? Don't talk to me about it. Smoke pouring out all day long. It covers the windows and paintwork. Can't have the windows open. Can't hang any washing out. Perhaps that Minister for the Environment would like to come and live in my house for a while. Then see if he still thinks it's moderate. 'Pearson's pong' my kids call it.'

3 The Wilthorpe Medical Officer of Health has issued the following press release:

```
                Pearson's Factory

Because of concern over alleged pollution
of the air and damage to health caused by
fumes from Pearson's factory on the edge of
the Prospect Hill estate, I have analysed
samples of air taken from points near the
factory and on streets in the estate.  The
results are as follows:
    Most of the gas given off is carbon
dioxide which does not smell, is not harmful
to health and is present in clean, natural
air.
    The necessary use of sulphur in one stage
of the manufacturing process does produce,
on one day of each week, a small quantity
of sulphur dioxide.  This has a strong smell,
but is not dangerous when dispersed in the
atmosphere.
    A small amount of soot is emitted, which
colours most of the smoke black, and settles
in moderate quantities on the area around
the factory.  It is not specifically bad
for health, though the general and long-
term effects are not good.
    I am in touch with Pearson's about ways
to reduce the amount of smoke emitted.
```

4 Pearson's Public Relations Officer has issued this statement:

```
            Pearson's look after the people

In consultation with the local Medical Officer,
Pearson's plan to install a special filter to
reduce the amount of smoke from their factory.
Though this is costly, Pearson's regard it as
essential.  Since there is no way of avoiding
the use of sulphur in the manufacturing process
on one day of each week, nothing can be done to
avoid the production of sulphur dioxide on that
day.  Pearson's factory provides jobs for 2,000
local residents, and its exports earn millions
of pounds for Great Britain each year.
```

What you have to do

Write a newspaper report on the subject of smoke and fumes coming from Pearson's factory at Wilthorpe.

Use as much of the information given as you think appropriate. You will, of course, need to rearrange and rewrite most of it and you will not be able to include it all, but try to represent each point of view fairly.

Remember that your answer is supposed to be a newspaper report. It must seize the attention of its readers. The usual way of doing this is to concentrate upon the aspect of public concern which makes an event newsworthy, and to emphasise it or dramatise it — by headings and sub-headings, by arranging the report in columns, in print of different sizes, and by providing photographs. In your report, you can do none of this, but you can supply a 'newsy' title and organise the facts to get the emphasis you need.

✳ Worked answer

Here is one way of beginning your report.

PEARSON'S POISON
Invitation to Minister

An angry housewife today invited Mr Reg Thomas, Minister for the Environment, to live in her house and sample 'Pearson's Poison'.

This is what local people call the yellow, sooty cloud of smoke from the Pearson's factory, which settles daily on houses and gardens in the Prospect Hill estate in the north of Wilthorpe. Windows stay shut. Washing cannot be hung out. Windows and paintwork suffer. And it smells.

Questioned by Mr Ackroyd, M.P. for Wilthorpe, Mr Thomas admitted that a moderate amount of unpleasant fumes was caused by vital industrial processes used at the factory. But no planning or environmental health regulations were being broken, and the management was trying to mitigate the health hazard. Pearson's had, he argued, brought two thousand jobs and prosperity to the town.

The Wilthorpe Medical Officer of Health claims that there is no need for alarm ...

Mark scheme

The purpose of the exercise is to sift the facts from the four different accounts, and to rewrite them in a different but consistent style.

Give yourself 10 marks for facts used.

Pearson's factory/which employs 2000 people/ at Wilthorpe/ emits smoke fumes/ over the Prospect Hill estate/ in the north of the town./The fumes smell/ and the smoke drops soot on houses and gardens./The fumes are sulphur dioxide/produced by burning sulphur./The fumes are harmless/though unpleasant./The soot has long-term effects on health./Wilthorpe's Medical Officer of Health is not worried/but is in touch with Pearson's/about filtering the smoke/though this is costly./The sulphur dioxide cannot be avoided/on one day of the week./Residents protesting ...

Give yourself a mark out of 10 for style, based on these five requirements:

- one coherent account, not four
- no direct copying except using quotation marks
- your own words
- skill in arranging facts
- 'newspaper' style — though accuracy expected

Add the two marks for a total out of 20.

17 Smash and grab raid

There has been a raid on Waterman's, a jeweller's shop in Mansfield Road, Stowmarket. As the first police officer to arrive on the scene after the raid, you take statements from three witnesses:

Mr Sid Collins (the shop manager)

It must have been about eleven, because I remember glancing at the clock as I was serving a customer a short time before and it was then ten to eleven. I suddenly heard this enormous crash. It sounded as if the room was falling down around us, but we all automatically looked towards the window. The funny thing was that at first I assumed that a car had actually crashed into the window. The burglar alarm didn't go off, because it is switched off during the day. If it wasn't, it would go off every time someone opened the door. I couldn't see much straightaway because the hardboard doors at the back of the display window were shut. So when I had collected my wits, I ran to the door. There is a button at the back of the counter that we can press to make the alarm go in the daytime, but in the heat of the moment I forgot to press it.

When I got to the door, I saw a man standing in the passage leading from the door to the street. The display windows are on both sides of it. As soon as he saw me, he raised a great big stick above his head. It was a pick-axe handle. Then he shouted, 'Get back in! Get back in!' I didn't have anything to defend myself with and I wasn't going to argue with a pick-axe handle, so I just shouted 'You get out!' and ran back into the shop.

I closed the door. Two or three customers and my assistant were standing still near the counter, staring at me. Then I heard the alarm bell go. My assistant had pressed the button. I didn't see what the man looked like because he had a stocking pulled over his face. Six of the display trays with the most expensive jewellery have gone. They didn't touch any of the cheaper stuff.

Mrs Rita Cross

I was looking in the window of the electrical shop next door when a loud screech of brakes made me look round, and there was this black van just skidding to a halt — one of those with doors at the back. A huge man carrying a stick and something heavy in a little sack jumped out and went towards Waterman's. He swung this little sack round in a circle two or three times to get a good speed up, and then let it go straight at the middle of Waterman's window. There was a terrific crash. Then suddenly there were two more men there, and they each had an enormous sack. They started picking great trays of things out of the window and putting them into their sacks. The man with the stick knocked a few big pieces of glass out of the window to help the other two, and then went and stood in the shop entrance. He had a stocking on his face. The other two didn't. They were shorter than the other man. One was young and thin. The other one was getting on a bit, about in his fifties I would say because his hair was grey. Then they dashed back and got in the back of the van while the one with the stick got in at the side and the van roared off. I just stood there. I couldn't move. I didn't try to shout. It was over so quick and everywhere seemed so quiet. Then the alarm bell started ringing. I didn't catch the number of the van.

Mr Carl Steadman

I was sitting in the car opposite the clothes shop waiting for my son, who was shopping. The van stopped in front of me, but I was tuning the radio and the first thing I heard was the crash. Someone screamed. There were three men all at Waterman's window, pulling glass out and stuffing things from the window into sacks. They must all have been youngsters by the speed they did the job and then scampered back to the van. They were not very tall, but the man with the stick and stocking, he was huge and didn't seem to hurry as much as the others. Once he had got in, they were off. The van was a black Transit, but I didn't think of taking the number. I looked as it went off, though, and I think it was a 'T' registration and I'm pretty sure the letters HE were in front of the numbers.

What you have to do

In these three accounts, you have information about what happened. Before detectives and forensic scientists start work, you have to present the officer in charge of this case with a report which simply gives the facts of what happened. You do this by combining the three accounts you have into a report. The witnesses say many things that the officer will not want to know, but at various points they do give the important facts and it is these you must concentrate on.

18 The man who planted trees

Read the information below and then write a report following the instructions at the end.

1 An extract from a geography book published in 1910:

The Alpine area of Provence is barren and arid, with nothing growing except wild lavender. The climate is harsh. A few abandoned villages are inhabited only by trappers, who lead a primitive existence.

2 An extract from a geography book published in 1955:

The Alpine region of Provence near Vergons has changed during this century. Previously a bare, desert region, it is now covered by oak forests and plantations of beech and birch. In 1913 Vergons had three inhabitants; it now has 30, including young families. New houses are surrounded by vegetable and flower gardens.

3 Entries in the records of the registrar at Banon, a town in Provence:

10 June, 1860   born Charles Bouffer, boy; father: T. Bouffer, sheep-farmer.

2 Sept., 1878   married, Charles Bouffer, sheep farmer, to Louise Coutte, seamstress.

4 April, 1880   born Paul Bouffer, boy; father: C. Bouffer, sheep-farmer.

14 April, 1889   died Paul Bouffer, boy, son of C. Bouffer; death due to scarlet fever.

15 July, 1895   died Louise Bouffer, wife of C. Bouffer; death due to heart attack.

10 Nov., 1947   died C. Bouffer, bee-keeper; death due to lung disease.

4 Entries from the diary of a mountain climber and walker:

10 August, 1913   — spent some time walking through the lowland hills in Provence — arid, bare region — only lavender and coarse grass — met a shepherd — 30 sheep — sheltered for night — told me he lived on his own — wife and son had died — next day went with him and his flock — took a bag of 100 acorns — extraordinary — planted them 2 miles from his cottage — told me in 3 years he had planted 100,000 — 10,000 now survived — thought the land needed trees — though not his land — he was the only inhabitant — wanted to plant beech and birch in the valleys — thought there was moisture under the surface.

20 August, 1922   — walking again in Provence — surprisingly, met same shepherd as in 1913 — Charles Bouffer — only 4 sheep now but 100 beehives — did not know about First World War — now has a forest 11 miles by 3 miles — 7-foot oaks, 5-foot beeches — wonderful — brooks flow — there are meadows, flowers, bushes.

11 June, 1945   — visited Charles Bouffer again — he knew of Second World War but ignored it — rarely speaks now — Vergons region is covered by forests, farms, maple groves, villages.

5 Part of a speech by a priest at Charles Bouffer's funeral at a hospice in Banon, 12 November 1947:

I had the most enormous respect for Charles, an old, uneducated peasant, who even lost the power of speech at the end of his life. He completed a work of immense proportions. As a sheep-farmer in the Provence lowlands, he survived the tragic deaths of his wife and young son. He then moved into the mountains to live alone, and simply to do what he thought was needed, to plant trees. It was not his land, but he did not care for property and ownership. He simply planted. From the hands and soul of this one man sprang forests. He lived unknown. A forest ranger in 1935 said the forest had grown naturally. What civil servant could dream of such perseverance and generosity? He ignored two world wars, wars which destroyed, not created. Regular toil, the vigorous mountain air, and, above all, peace and serenity of spirit, gave him long life and excellent health. With only his own physical and moral resources, he turned ruined hamlets into thriving villages and barren landscape into healthy, productive farmland. He showed that man can be as effective as God in realms other than destruction.

What you have to do

Using the information given above, write for a magazine called *Conservation Now* a short biography of, and tribute to, Charles Bouffer. As different sources of material are used, information is repeated, but you should avoid repetition and make the basis of your account straightforward and chronological.

19 Religion

This is a discussion in which four senior pupils express some of their ideas about religion. Read it and then, following the instructions below, write a report.

'Were you in assembly this morning when the Head asked us to pray for Rob Wilkins?' asked Sean.

'Do you mean that boy who is very ill in hospital?' asked Debbie.

'Yes, I'm not going to, though. My Dad says it's silly praying to God to change the course of Nature. If anyone is as ill as Rob is, he'll only be cured by the scientists discovering a new "wonder" drug. I think it's a matter of medical science whether people are cured or not. Doctors and scientists can explain everything.'

'I'm not sure that they can,' replied Debbie. 'They're finding out new facts every day, and sometimes what they find out contradicts what they thought before. I think they're only discovering more about God's creation.'

'I agree with Sean,' interrupted Paul. 'I would rather trust the scientists than something I don't understand. If the creation is so wonderful, why is it so mysterious, and why does it need so much discovering? Anyway, if you pray for someone to get well, what about those who don't get well? Does that mean your prayers aren't answered? Scientists say that the world began as a big mass of gas, and I believe them.'

'Yes. I think that just about everything in the Bible is one big, long fairy story.' Now Sean was joining in again. 'What proof does anyone have that things happened exactly as it says?'

'That's just it,' cut in Gerry. He had only just joined the group and they all spun round to listen. 'You want proof of religion just as you want proof in Science or Maths, don't you? Can't you see that they're different? You've got to have faith to accept the truths of religion. You can't just do it by scientific proof. I don't think that the things we're taught in Science and Religious Studies are opposed to each other. You were saying only the other day that you believe in ghosts and spirits and telepathy. You see, you accept some things you don't understand, but not religion.'

'All right,' mumbled Paul. 'I can see what you're getting at. But it still seems funny to me that God allows wars, famines, earthquakes, floods and illness to happen all over the world.'

'I'll tell you one thing that annoys me, though,' said Sean, 'and that's the way parents behave. They send us to Sunday school and church, but never go themselves. They say they haven't got time.'

'I quite agree there,' said Gerry, and Debbie also nodded her approval. 'They've got no time for church until they want to get married or buried. They always seem to want those two services conducted in church.'

At last, everyone agreed.

What you have to do

The editor of the school magazine has asked you to write a report of this discussion and to entitle it 'Some pupils' opinions about religion'. This means that, without writing in dialogue (or speech) form, and without using the pupils' exact words, you should give a true account of their ideas. Be careful not to add any of your own ideas, however strongly you may feel.

20 Rent strike

Imagine that you are a local government officer in the Housing Department of Belston District Council in Yorkshire. You have to prepare a special report for the next meeting of the Housing Committee of the Council on Catherine Street. You have gathered the following information:

- The Rent Collection Department has told you that there are rent arrears of £3,000 for the whole of Belston, and that half of this is owed by tenants in Catherine Street. The Rent Department wants to employ a debt collection agency for Catherine Street.

- Tenants say that they are on a 'rent strike' because the Council will not repair their homes. They complain about: damp on bedroom walls — plaster crumbling — rooms that cannot be properly decorated — badly fitting doors — some windows that do not shut properly — other windows that will never open — part of a ceiling that has collapsed because of damp — leaking roofs — entire houses having only two electric points — paper peeling off walls because of damp — an electric water heater that is not repaired.

- The Works Department of the Council, which has responsibility for the maintenance of houses, makes the following points: Catherine Street tenants treat their houses badly — some keep coal in the kitchen — garden gates have been removed and disposed of — cars are parked on front gardens — some structural alterations inside the houses have been made by the tenants themselves without asking permission — building materials are expensive, hard to get, and take a long time to be delivered.

What you have to do

Write the report in clear, correct sentences, arranging the above material as you think appropriate.

21 The price of bread

This is a special press release sent by Berry's, a national grocery chain, to the editors of all the national daily newspapers.

> Berry & Co. wish to announce that they plan to maintain the present retail price of a sliced loaf of bread at 50p for at least the next twelve months, in spite of the effects of European Economic Community agricultural policy on our wheat prices.

This is what a spokesperson at the Ministry of Agriculture said when asked to comment on the matter:

> 'I am pleased to learn of this attempt to maintain a stable price level for such a basic and important item of food.'

This is what the Managing Director of Sunshine Bread, the third most important bakers in the country, said at a recent interview:

> The wholesale price of bread is bound to rise soon by at least 2p per loaf. The cost of wheat and therefore of flour is soaring because of the European Common Agricultural Policy. British farmers are limited in the number of acres of wheat they can grow, so this shortage of supply is bound to result in higher prices.

The General Secretary of the National Union of Farmers has recently written in a national magazine:

> 'British farmers are so restricted in their production of wheat by bureaucratic orders from Brussels that they will have to raise their prices considerably.'

What you have to do

As the Secretary of the Nationwide Consumers' Society, write a report for a magazine called *The Baker* arguing that the price of bread should be kept stable.

22 Dangerous toys

You work in the quality control section of Playmac, manufacturers of children's toys. You have recently received complaints about some of your products:

- Bears and dogs whose eyes come out easily and are attached to the end of a long, sharp pin
- Dolls whose arms come off to expose a sharp steel pin to which they were attached
- Lorries which are made partly of plastic and partly of steel, and have sharply pointed angles
- A plastic disc which spins between two threads — when spinning above a certain speed, it splits into many fragments which disperse in all directions
- A 'space gun' which makes a high-pitched whine and frightens small children
- Dolls' make-up which causes a rash when children inevitably get it on their own skin

What you have to do

Write a report to the Managing Director of Playmac, pointing out the seriousness of the above faults and suggesting that they are put right.

LETTERS

There are two main types of letter: the personal letter and the formal or business letter.

Personal letters

This is an example of a personal letter.

86 Beech Gardens,
Rainford,
Shrewsbury,
Salop,
SH8 2DN.
4th April 1986

Dear Tracey,

Thanks for your letter which came last week, in which you said that you are representing Avon in the National Schools' Athletic Championships at Shrewsbury on Saturday 24th May - congratulations! As you know, the following week is half term, and my parents said that I could invite you to stay with us for a few days.

I would love to watch you run in your event. Do you think it would be a good idea if Dad came to fetch us in the car afterwards? Then could you stay at least until Tuesday? We are supposed to revise for our exams in that week, of course, but two or three days off at the beginning of the holiday won't make any difference.

Mum and Dad send their love and they hope you and your parents have settled down in Bristol. Write again soon.

I can't wait to see you.

Best wishes,
Helen.

Business letters

33 Grantham Road,
Waddington,
LINCOLN,
LN3 4PU.

5th June 1986

The Sales Manager,
Direct Mail Record Company,
Shepley Street,
Audenshaw,
Greater Manchester,
MU4 CB1.

Dear Sir/Madam,

Thank you for your letter saying that the double album 'Road Songs' by the group 'Wanderlust', which I ordered from you, is no longer obtainable. Thank you also for returning my postal order.

I was not surprised that you did not have 'Road Songs' in stock, because it was recorded several years ago. However, I am sure that you will have their latest LP, 'Songs from the Wild Side'. Would you please send me a copy?

As I do not know the price of this record, please enclose your invoice and bill for postage and packing, and I will send you a postal order by return of post.

Yours faithfully,

MDSmith

M.D. Smith

There are two ways of setting out business letters. On the opposite page is a 'fully-blocked' letter (everything starting at the left-hand margin); below is a 'semi-blocked' letter. Both the fully-blocked and the semi-blocked styles are acceptable for business letters. The fully-blocked style is easier to use on a word-processor.

33 Grantham Road,
Waddington,
LINCOLN,
LN3 4PU.

20th June 1986

The Sales Manager,
Direct Mail Record Company,
Shepley Street,
Audenshaw,
Greater Manchester,
MU4 CB1.

Dear Sir/Madam,

Thank you for sending me 'Songs from the Wild Side' by 'Wanderlust', which I ordered in my letter dated 5th June 1986.

I enclose your invoice and bill for postage and packing, with a postal order for £5.95. Please send a receipt.

Thank you again for such prompt service.

Yours faithfully,

M DSmith

M.D. Smith

Points to remember

- Write the date in full, i.e. 15th (or 15) March 1988, rather than in figures (15.3.88).

Personal Letters (see page 59)

- The tone of the letter should be friendly and chatty, but avoid using slang.
- In an invitation, be careful to include all the necessary information — place, date, and time.
- Do not use letter clichés, e.g. 'I am just dropping you a line', or 'I must close now'.
- A number of endings are possible. 'Yours truly', 'Yours sincerely', or 'Yours affectionately' are fairly formal. You can use endings like 'Best wishes', or 'Kind regards' in letters to people you know well.

Business letters (see page 60)

- Remember to include the full name and address of the company you are writing to.
  Abbreviations such as 'Co.' (Company), 'Ltd' (Limited), or 'plc' (Public Limited Company — alternatives are p.l.c., P.L.C., PLC) are acceptable. Try to write them as the company does.
- If you do not know the name of the person to whom you are writing, begin your letter 'Dear Sir/Madam'. If there is no special person to whom you can refer your letter, write 'Dear Sirs'. A letter to the editor of a newspaper or magazine usually opens with the greeting, 'Sir'.
- It is a good idea to start your letter with a reference to what it is about, e.g.

  <u>Your invoice of 19 February</u>

- The tone of a business letter should be formal but polite. Remember to include all the necessary information. Your letter should provide a record of any matters being discussed.
- Do not use formal jargon, e.g. 'I beg to acknowledge receipt of your communication of the 15th inst.' Just say, 'Thank you for your letter of 15 March.'

- The ending: If you use a name in the greeting, the ending must be 'Yours sincerely'. If 'Sir/Madam' or 'Sirs', the ending must be 'Yours faithfully'.
- The signature usually consists only of the writer's name. If any title, such as 'Mr', 'Ms', 'Mrs' or 'Miss', is added, it should be placed in brackets after the signature. The position of the writer can be added below the signature.

A few tips

When you are doing the exercises that follow, try to remember these points:

- Use every fact or idea in the information given, because in the mark scheme each fact or idea will carry a mark.
- Do not simply copy the points from the question but rephrase them in your own words. Be fluent, though not long-winded, because some marks will be awarded for tone and style.
- Where the sender's address is not supplied, make up an appropriate one.
- Provide a suitable introductory paragraph to the subject.
- Try to give an appropriate, natural conclusion.
- Write a rough draft before your final answer.

23 The good Samaritan

This exercise has been done for you, as a guide.

Imagine that you are a mother or father whose eleven-year-old daughter, Angie, has just arrived home on the bus after a trip into town. She explains that when she was on the bus she discovered that she had lost the money you gave her for her fare. When she explained this to the conductor, a stranger paid her fare and did not tell her his name. You are so grateful to the stranger that you write to the local newspaper to thank him, hoping that he will read the letter.

The following points are relevant:

1 The bus was crowded and no one else offered.
2 You think he was as generous as 'the good Samaritan' described in the Bible.
3 If Angie had been put off the bus she would have had to walk five miles home.
4 Angie was so relieved that she cried when she got home.
5 You would have been very worried if she had had to walk.
6 She has recently been ill and is not very strong.
7 If she had been late, she would have missed a music lesson for which you would have had to pay.
8 You would like to repay the money.

✳ Worked answer

Here is the letter that Angie's mother or father might have written to the editor of the local newspaper.

11 Burton Street,
Cambridge,
Cambs,
CB32 4HT.
21 September 1986

The Editor,
'The Cambridge Daily News',
27 St Andrew's Street,
Cambridge,
Cambs,
CB1 3LR.

Sir,

    Would you give me space to praise an act of generosity and thoughtfulness by a member of the general public?

    Recently, my daughter Angie, aged eleven, was on the bus going home, when she discovered that she had lost her fare-money. A stranger, overhearing her explanation to the conductor, paid her fare.

    The alternative to the bus ride was a five-mile walk home. Her lateness would have caused me considerable worry and she would have missed her music lesson. She has, moreover, recently suffered an illness which has left her rather weak.

    The stranger did not tell Angie his name, and so I hope that he may read this letter and know of my sincere thanks. Angie cried with relief. Of course, I would like to repay the money if the gentleman would care to get in touch with me.

    Meanwhile, it is comforting to know that amid the selfishness, violence and greed of our modern society, there exist such 'Good Samaritans' as this public-spirited gentleman.

Yours faithfully,

Marlene King

Marlene King

Mark Scheme

Out of a total of 20 marks, 10 are for content, that is, for reference to each of the eight points in the information given, as these are all relevant to the purpose of the letter. Points 1 and 6 each carry 2 marks.

There are 5 marks for layout. One mark is lost for each major error, such as no date, addresses in the wrong position, or the wrong form of signature. The remaining 5 marks are awarded for the style in which the points have been rephrased, and for the general tone and fluency of the letter, especially in the introduction and the conclusion.

24 Traffic hazards

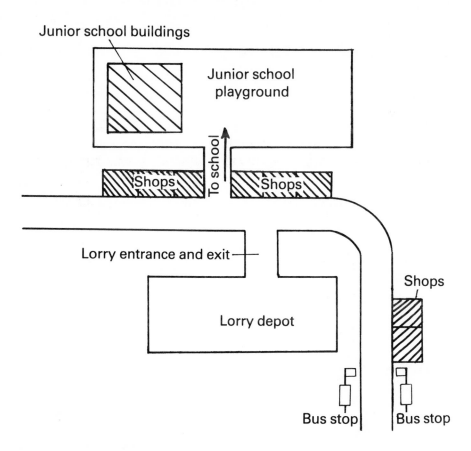

Junior school buildings

Junior school playground

Shops

To school

Shops

Lorry entrance and exit

Lorry depot

Shops

Bus stop

Bus stop

The diagram shows a main road at the end of a village. Through most of the village, the road has a 30 m.p.h. speed limit, but for the section shown the limit is 40 m.p.h. As the parent of two children aged seven and nine, who attend the junior school, you think this is dangerous for these reasons:

- Cars can park by the shops near the school entrance
- Heavy lorries use an entrance opposite — they are slow-moving and cause traffic to build up behind them
- Drivers of cars coming from the direction of the bus stop cannot see the lorries until they nearly run into them

- People using the shops opposite the bus stop have to cross the road near the bend if they use the bus
- Cars can park near the shops opposite the bus stop.

What you have to do

Using your own name, write a letter from your address, which is 5 Chaucer Road, Gosthorpe, Northants. Address the letter to: The Editor, Northants Echo, Central Hall Square, Northampton, NN1 4PU. Briefly express your concern about the safety of school-children, shoppers and motorists, and argue that, among other improvements to this stretch of road, the most urgent is the reduction of the speed limit to 30 m.p.h.

You should take care to set out your letter in a formal style.

25 Applying for a job

This exercise, which has been done for you, asks you to write a letter applying for a job.

Remember the following points:

1 Make the style clear and polite.
2 If you are replying to an advertisement, state the publication in which you saw the advertisement.
3 State clearly the position for which you are applying, as there may be several vacancies at that firm.
4 Give details of your age, schools attended, any examination successes you have had and prospective examination entries.
5 Give details of your current job, even a part-time job, if you already have one.
6 Say why the job attracts you and give information about relevant experience you have had or interests you have.
7 Stress the qualities you have which you consider make you suitable for the job.
8 Give the names and addresses of referees, that is, people who will answer questions about you or will write on your behalf. You must first obtain their permission.

What you have to do

Write a letter of application for the post described above. Refer to examinations you have taken, giving the results, and examinations you are now taking with expected results. Refer to as many of the points made in the advertisement as you think appropriate. Send the letter from your home address. You should take care to set out your letter in a formal style.

✳Worked answer

On the opposite page is the letter that might have been written by someone applying for this job.

3 Sandringham Road,
Dereham,
Norfolk,
NR47 5LE.

Director of Personnel,   4th April 1986
Bowyer's Ltd,
Norwich,
Norfolk,
NR3 1GR.

Dear Sir,

Retailing Trainees

I wish to apply for the position of Trainee in Retailing, advertised in the 'Eastern Daily Press' of 3rd April 1986.

I am a fifth-year pupil at Dereham High School. I was sixteen on 23rd February. Next term, I will be sitting examinations in Maths, Economics, English Language, English Literature, Science, History, French and Computer Studies at GCSE level. I have not passed any public examinations yet, but in the trial examinations held at school last December, I achieved the equivalent of Grade 'C' in Maths and Economics and Grade 'B' in English Language, Science and Computer Studies. I achieved Grade 'D' in the other three subjects.

I am very keen to begin a career in retailing. I enjoy meeting people and am told that I have a pleasant personality. If I succeeded in securing this position, I would, of course, be most anxious to study all the different aspects of the retail business.

For the past six months I have been working every Saturday at Lipway's supermarket, 3, High Street, Dereham. I enjoy this job very much. The Manager, Mr A. Christie, says he is willing to answer any enquiry about me, and you may refer to him if you wish. You may also refer to my Headmaster, Mr T. Saunders, at Dereham High School, Chaucer Road, Dereham.

I trust that this information is of assistance to you in your consideration of my application.

Yours faithfully,

Andy Marks

Andy Marks

26 More jobs

SITUATIONS VACANT

> **A SALES PERSON** is required by
> a new and rapidly expanding
> shoe company. Sales experience
> not essential as training will be
> given to suitably smart, intelligent
> young person.
> Apply The Manager,
> Northampton Shoe Co. Ltd,
> Bond Street, Northampton,
> NN1 3PR.

A FULL-TIME WAGES CLERK
is required by the Williams Group.
$37^1/_2$ hours per week.
Good rate of pay.
Typing ability would be useful.
Apply Accounts Manager,
Williams Group of Companies,
Lawn Road, Nottingham,
NG22 6ST.

What you have to do

1 You are the Manager of *one* of the companies above and have the vacancy described for a young school-leaver. You write a letter to the Youth Employment Officer of the town asking him or her to suggest a suitable person for *one* of the posts — a person with the qualifications and character you want.

2 Write a letter of application for *one* of the jobs.

27 Television sport

This exercise has been done for you as an example of a letter arguing a point of view.

At your school there has been a debate on the topic, 'There is too much sport on television'. The following points were made in support of this motion, i.e. against having so much sport on television.

1 It is unhealthy to sit in armchairs and watch sport.
2 Professional sport needs people to go and pay to watch it; otherwise it cannot carry on.
3 Watching sport is a substitute for playing it, and all sorts of sports will die for lack of people taking part.
4 Only competitive sports are televised, not purely recreational ones.
5 Television conveys only the competitive aspects of any sport, not the real fun of doing it.
6 Commentators get on your nerves, telling you what to think and how to react.
7 Selecting which sport is televised gives the producers far too much power to promote or neglect certain sports.
8 Most televised sport is already sponsored by advertisers.

These points were made against the motion, i.e. saying that there is not too much sport on television.

1 Televised sport gives great pleasure to millions of followers of such sports as football, cricket, horse racing, wrestling, motor racing, athletics, rugby, snooker, darts, boxing, tennis, golf.

2 People who could not afford the transport or entrance money to see these sports can watch them.

3 People who are too ill or too old to go out to see sports can watch them.

4 You often have a better view on television than you would if you were there.

5 The commentators give you more information than you would have if you attended in person.

6 The voice of the commentator contributes to the excitement.

7 Particular programmes usually give you some experts' views on a special event, and you would not get this if you attended.

8 Television inspires many people to take up sports that they would not otherwise know about.

9 Watching the best competitors and players helps to improve the viewer's own skill and knowledge.

10 It is possible to watch a much greater range of different sports on television than it is to attend in person.

What you have to do

Write to the editor of *Radio Times* either arguing that there is too much sport on television, *or* arguing *against* someone who has written to say that there is too much.

Write from your home address. *Radio Times* is at 35 Marylebone High Street, London, W1M 4AA.

You should take care to set out your letter in a formal style.

The editor is more likely to publish your letter if you write briefly.

21 Watson Road,
Goole,
Humberside,
HU73 2TL.

21st April 1986

The Editor,
'Radio Times',
35 Marylebone High Street,
LONDON,
W1M 4AA.

Sir,

I am writing to protest about the amount of sport that is televised by the BBC.

If we take last Saturday as an example, BBC 1 transmitted programmes for $17\frac{1}{2}$ hours. Of this, 'Grandstand' occupied $4\frac{1}{2}$ hours during the afternoon, covering soccer, snooker, racing, horse trials and rugby. 'Match of the Day' lasted for $\frac{3}{4}$ hour in the evening. This makes a total of $5\frac{1}{4}$ hours. BBC 2 began the same day with 9 hours of Open University programmes. As this is a highly specialised series for a tiny viewing public, we may discount it, and consider the 10 hours from 3 p.m. Of this, there were $\frac{3}{4}$ hour of horse trials, 1 hour of rugby and 3 hours of snooker, making $4\frac{3}{4}$ hours. Surely to have 30% of BBC1's output and nearly half of that of BBC 2 consisting entirely of sport, is excessive.

Not everyone shares this degree of interest in sport, and the BBC should provide a public service for the whole population, not a section of it. But even for sports fans, one wonders what purpose televised sport serves. Sport is to take part in, not to watch. To sit and watch from an armchair is not the most healthy activity. It can be bad for the chest and circulation. Those who do a lot of it could have heart attacks while still young. Any particular sport survives only as long as people participate, and professional sport needs paying spectators.

Only competitive sports make good television. The type of sport that is enjoyed for itself is obviously not worth televising. There are more anglers than footballers in this country, but they do not enjoy — or suffer from — television coverage.

The fact that only some sports are televised, of course, gives the producers the power to promote some sports — for instance, darts, snooker and bowls in recent years — and ignore others, such as squash, archery or badminton. Of course, when people attend sports occasions, they reflect on them as they wish, without the disadvantage of a commentator shouting in their ears, telling them what to think.

Finally, I would like to anticipate the arguments of those who praise television companies for the money they put into sport. The money television pays is but a drop in the ocean, compared to the true paying supporters of sport, the paying public and the commercial sponsors.

For all of these reasons, I wish television would stick to its main functions of information and entertainment, and leave sports enthusiasts to get out of their armchairs and join in, for the sake of their own health — and the sport they supposedly follow.

Yours faithfully,

Z. Thompson

Z. Thompson

28 Blood sports

Imagine that you have attended a meeting of the 'PABS' organisation, the full title of which is 'Party Against Blood Sports'. At the meeting the following points were made:

1 There are 336 hunts in England. The 'sport' consists of chasing and killing foxes. This is quite legal.
2 At the end of most hunts, the fox is torn to pieces by the hounds.
3 There are estimated to be 1800 farmers and landowners in England who rent out 'shooting rights' to friends, whom they invite to shoot rabbits, hares, grouse, partridges, pheasants and wood pigeons. This shooting is also legal.
4 Rabbits, hares, and game birds are often injured by being shot and not killed humanely.
5 Badger-digging, otter-hunting and even cock-fighting and deer-hunting occur in various parts of England and all these are quite illegal and cause untold suffering.
6 There are more efficient and humane ways of killing foxes, rabbits and deer than hunting or shooting.
7 Otters are nearly extinct and badgers need protection.

8 Cock-fighting, extremely cruel, is quickly dealt with by police if they discover it, and it exists only for gambling.

9 At issue are not only the cruelty inflicted by blood sports, but people's lack of dignity and irresponsibility towards the wildlife they can easily control.

You have also read a pamphlet published by 'SPORT', the Society for the Preservation of Rural Traditions, which makes the following points.

1 Otter-hunting, deer-hunting and cock-fighting are illegal and not supported by SPORT.

2 Foxes are pests that do much damage to farm animals and need to be controlled.

3 Hunting is better for controlling the numbers of foxes than shooting or poisoning.

4 Rabbits and hares do great harm to farmers' crops.

5 Shooting rabbits and hares is much less cruel, and more efficient, than trapping or poisoning.

6 Badgers need to be exterminated where they spread tuberculosis among cattle.

7 Wild pigeons eat great quantities of farmers' grain and must be controlled.

8 Game, partridges and pheasants are specially bred to be shot, and if they were not artificially protected by game-keepers before the shooting season begins, their numbers would greatly reduce.

9 Most people who object to hunting eat meat and poultry.

10 This meat and poultry has been bred, often in cramped conditions, only to be killed and eaten by people.

What you have to do

Write a letter from your home address to the editor of a magazine called *Rural England* supporting the point of view of *either* PABS *or* SPORT. The address of the magazine is 17 Taunton Avenue, Camden, London, NW3 2RP. You should take care to set out your letter in a formal style. Remember that magazine editors like letters to be reasonably brief and concise.

29 Bad neighbours

This exercise has been done for you as an example of a letter of complaint.

You live in a semi-detached house. Your neighbours annoy you — not the neighbours who live in the house adjoining yours, but those whose house is separated from yours by your two drive-ways. Things have got so bad that you decide to write to the local Department of Environmental Health, mentioning the following points.

1 Mr Mitchell, your neighbour, has two Alsatian dogs which he very rarely takes out for exercise.
2 Both Mr and Mrs Mitchell go out to work all day and shut the dogs in the garage, where they bark most of the time.
3 At other times, such as when visitors or the postman or milkman call, the dogs are noisy when they are in the drive and garden.
4 They have so frightened your two small children, aged five and two, that you have had to erect a six-foot high fence between the two houses.

5 The dogs constantly foul the Mitchells' driveway, causing an offensive smell.

6 You have tried to discuss the matter with Mr Mitchell but this has caused only shouting and bad feeling on his part.

7 To annoy you further, he leaves a powerful portable radio playing loudly in the driveway at weekends.

8 You sometimes work on night shift, and need to sleep during the day, but are prevented from doing so by the dogs.

What you have to do

Write a letter to the Department of Environmental Health, using the information you have been given to point out that this situation is badly affecting the peace of mind and the physical health of yourself and your family.

Address your letter to the Chief Inspector of Environmental Health. The Department's address is: Department of Environmental Health, Civic Buildings, St Peter's Square, Scunthorpe, South Humberside, DN24 3NH.

Your address is: 16 Chichester Road, Brigg, South Humberside, DN45 3AH.

You should take care to set out your letter in a formal style.

You will probably make a better impression on the Chief Inspector if you make your points fairly briefly.

16 Chichester Road,
Brigg,
South Humberside,
DN45 3AH.

23rd April 1986

Chief Inspector,
Department of Environmental Health,
Civic Buildings,
St Peter's Square,
Scunthorpe,
South Humberside,
DN24 3NH.

Dear Sir,

No. 18 Chichester Road

I wish to make a formal complaint that Mr Mitchell, my neighbour, is damaging the peace of mind and physical health of my family.

The house in which we live at the address above is semi-detached, and Mr Mitchell lives at No. 18. Our houses are separated by our two driveways. He owns two Alsatian dogs which are rarely exercised, but spend all day shut in the garage, barking. They make a lot of noise when the postman and milkman or other visitors call.

My two children, aged five and two, are so frightened of them that I have had to build a six-foot high fence between the two driveways and gardens. The smell caused by the dogs' excrement on the driveway is terrible. Mr Mitchell refuses to discuss the matter, and has simply shouted abuse when I have approached him. He also annoys me by playing a port-able radio loudly at weekends. Apart from the nuisance caused to my family, I lose sleep because of all this, as I sometimes work on night shift, but am prevented by the dogs from sleeping during the day.

In view of Mr Mitchell's conduct, I have to ask you to pursue this matter further with him.

Yours faithfully,

Denise Bennett

Denise Bennett

30 Leisure centre

Imagine that a very big leisure centre has been opened in Welham. It has cost many millions of pounds to build, and the local population has been saying for years that it is just what the town needs. It contains an ice rink, a swimming pool, two squash courts, a sports hall for badminton, tennis, basketball, table tennis, archery and judo, a bowling alley, a snooker and billiards room and a refreshment area and bar. It has been open for a year during which you have heard the following complaints:

1 In the ice rink, older 'experts' speed round, causing danger and injury to children who are learning
2 One squash court always seems to be closed and there is always a queue for the other
3 There is no proper booking system for the table tennis, and people simply push in
4 The vending machines in the refreshment area are often empty
5 The whole building is closed most Saturday evenings for social events, using the sports hall as a dance floor and bar
6 The swimming pool and the sports hall are closed to the public so that private clubs can use them for too many sessions
7 The snooker and billiards room is so full of youngsters larking about on the tables that there is no room for anyone wanting a serious game
8 The admission charge of £1.00 for adults and 70p for children is too high when there is also a separate charge for each facility.

What you have to do

Write a fairly brief formal letter to the Manager of Welham Leisure Centre, Chelmsford Road, Welham, Essex, CH5 4ET, informing him of the above complaints and suggesting remedies. Remember to include your home address which, of course, needs to be in Welham.

You should take care to set out your letter in a formal style.

31 Camping accident

You are a teacher who is taking a party of 20 boys on a camping holiday in the Lake District. One of the boys, Neil Marston, fell and broke his collar-bone during an unofficial football game that the boys had organised on the camping field. He has been treated at the casualty department of the local hospital, and the doctor has said that he can continue to stay at the camp for the remainder of the week and does not need to go home, or stay at the hospital.

The following points are relevant to Neil's situation:

1 He is in some discomfort but no great pain.
2 The bone has been set and he has to have his arm in a high sling to relieve stress on the collar bone.
3 He wants to stay at the camp and go home in the bus with all the others.
4 The doctor at the hospital says he can stay at the camp.
5 He is not to go climbing or on any strenuous expeditions.

6 You have no car, as you came in the bus with the boys. You are willing, however, to take Neil to the nearest railway station and buy him a ticket home if his mother wishes.

7 This happened on Wednesday evening. Neil fell over a large stone in the field. No one was to blame. It was an accident.

8 It is now Thursday morning. The whole party is to pack up and go home on Saturday morning.

9 There are many ways in which Neil can be useful around the camp for the last two days of the holiday.

10 He is in good spirits.

What you have to do

Neil's mother is not on the telephone. Write her a letter explaining exactly what has happened to Neil.

Your advice is that Neil should stay at the camp and go home in the bus with the rest of the boys, but say that the final decision is hers. Try not to make Mrs Marston too anxious, but make the relevant points clear.

Your address is St Luke's Camp, Grayrigg, Kendal, Cumbria, KE4 6HJ.

Mrs Marston lives at 32 Orchard Rise, Stockbridge, Hampshire, WN41 6JV.

32 Youth hostelling

As the Secretary of Oxford Road Youth Club, Sheringham, Norfolk, NR6 7AL, you have received a letter from the warden of Lakeview Abbey Youth Hostel. He complains that after a group from your club had left:

- The table had two sets of initials carved in the top surface — he is sure that they had not been there before
- A leg of one of the chairs at the table was broken and two others were badly weakened
- Four books — from a small selection for guests to read — were missing

What you have to do

Write a letter in reply, making the tone as tactful as you can, in which you admit responsibility for the damage and for the loss of the books. You offer to pay compensation and promise to seek out the culprits and deal with them according to the rules of the club. The hostel is situated in Ambleside, Cumbria.

You received the letter on 3 August. Your reply should bear the club's address.

33 Camping holiday

Imagine that you are planning to take a group of eight youngsters, aged between fourteen and sixteen, on a hiking and camping holiday in a mountainous area of West Scotland. At present, the group is made up of three girls and three boys, so you need one more boy and one more girl to complete it. No more of your personal friends want to go. You have therefore appealed to the leader of a local youth club to recommend someone and she has, quite confidentially, given you the names of two boys and two girls who, she is sure, would like to go. She has sent the following notes on their characteristics and interests so that you can choose the boy and girl you think most suitable.

Donald

Main interest is football — a regular attender of the youth club — very popular and sociable — health is often not good — much time away from school because of colds and infectious illnesses — no experience of camping.

James

No interest in sport — reserved and quiet, does not mix too well — only rarely attends youth club — interested in wildlife and the countryside — keen member of local natural history society — very fit and strong — has never been ill or away from school — has been camping with his family.

Pat

A popular girl — very good at swimming, tennis and hockey — likes all kinds of music including 'pop' — attends other youth clubs and goes to dances at local sports and social clubs — says that what she most hates is being on her own.

Jane

Shy, retiring girl who always stays close to one particular friend when she attends the youth club — reads a lot — likes classical music — loves walking in the countryside — detests all sports.

What you have to do

Choose which boy and which girl you think will be most suitable to join your group on this holiday.

Taking care to set out the letter properly, and addressing her as 'Dear Ms Conroy', write a letter to the Youth Club leader telling her the boy and the girl whom you would like her to invite. The letter is confidential, and will not be read by any of the boys and girls. Referring to her notes, give her as full an explanation as possible of your choice. Thank her for her help and make your general tone friendly and polite. Do not write too much. Make up suitable addresses for yourself and the youth club leader.

Postscript

1 Read this example of a formal letter.

```
                                32 Jay Lane,
                                Margate,
                                KENT,
                                CT37 8LJ.

                                28th June 1986

   The Sales Manager,
   Trifix plastic Plc,
   Exeter,
   DEVON,
   EX3 8JD.

   Dear Sir,
        I notice that in your current
   catalogue you advertise a model of the
   American space shuttle.

        Nothing in the catalogue says that
   this is not yet available, yet the manager
   of my local model shop, from which I have
   obtained all my other models, says that he
   does not stock it because it does not exist.

        Would you please let me know whether
   this is at present for sale and, if so,
   whether I may order it by post and pay for
   it by cheque. I expect that you will
   require an additional payment for postage
   and packing.

        I look forward to your reply.

                      Yours faithfully,

                      T. Rollinson

                      T. Rollinson (Mr)
```

What you have to do

Without looking back at the pages which introduced the Letters section of this book, list the points to remember for the business style of letter layout, using the model above.

2 Read this example of a personal letter.

13 Braganza Street,
London,
SE17 0JX.
7th November 1986

Dear Steve,
     How's it going down there in Swindon? Moving in here was a laugh. The new school's all right – I'm in the first team already, which must say something about the rest of them!
     I've made a few mates but as yet there's nothing like the old gang. I suppose all that will take time. The big news is that I managed a ride on the next door neighbour's Harley Davidson last Saturday. Of course it's nowhere in comparison with the S-reg Honda 50 that delivers me to school in immaculate style every day. Still, we can dream, can't we? By the time Easter gets around my new-found wealth as a Saturday morning shelf-filler might have bought me a Superdream. We'll just have to wait and see, won't we?
     Let me know how it's all going.
     All the best,
       Dave

What you have to do

Without looking back at the pages which introduced the Letters section of this book, list the points to remember for the personal style of letter layout, using the model above.